FIGHTING CYBERCRIME:
AT THE LOCAL, REGIONAL
AND INTERNATIONAL LEVELS

Dr. NASSER AFIFY

2018

TABLE OF CONTENTS

CHAPTER ONE: INTRODUCTION ……………………….. 1

CHAPTER TWO: EVOLUTION OF CYBERCRIME……………9

CHAPTER THREE: A LEGAL PERSPECTIVE OF CYBERCRIME……………………………………………….23

CHAPTER FOUR: INTERNATIONAL INSTRUMENTS FOR COMBATING CYBERCRIME………………………………45

CHAPTER FIVE: CYBERCRIME AND COMPUTER CRIME LEGISLATION………………………………………………72

CONCLUSION………………………………………………80

REFERENCES………………………………………………81

CHAPTER ONE

INTRODUCTION

Cybercrime is defined as a crime in which a computer is the object of the crime (hacking, phishing, spamming) or is used as a tool to commit an offense (child pornography, hate crimes). Cybercriminals may use computer technology to access personal information, business trade secrets or use the internet for exploitative or malicious purposes. Criminals can also use computers for communication and document or data storage. Criminals who perform these illegal activities are often referred to as hackers. Cybercrime may also be referred to as computer crime.

'Definitions' of cybercrime mostly depend upon the purpose of using the term. A limited number of acts against the confidentiality, integrity and availability of computer data or systems represent the core of cybercrime. Beyond this, however, computer-related acts for personal or financial gain or harm, including forms of identity-related crime, and computer content-related acts (all of which fall within a wider meaning of the term 'cybercrime') do not lend themselves easily to efforts to arrive at legal definitions of the aggregate term. Certain definitions are required for the core of cybercrime acts.

However, a 'definition' of cybercrime is not as relevant for other purposes, such as defining the scope of specialized investigative and international cooperation powers, which are better focused on electronic evidence for any crime, rather than a broad, artificial 'cybercrime' construct.

Cybercrime is any criminal activity that involves a computer, networked device or a network. While most cybercrimes are carried out in order to generate profit for the cybercriminals, some cybercrimes are carried out against computers or devices directly to damage or disable them, while others use computers or networks to spread malware, illegal information, images or other materials. Some cybercrimes do both -- i.e., target computers to infect them with viruses, which are then spread to other machines and, sometimes, entire networks.

Cybercrime is criminal activity done using computers and the Internet. This includes anything from downloading illegal music files to stealing millions of dollars from online bank accounts. Cybercrime also includes non-monetary offenses, such as creating and distributing viruses on other computers or posting confidential business information on the Internet.

Perhaps the most prominent form of cybercrime is identity theft, in which criminals use the Internet to steal personal information from other users. Two of the most common ways this is done is through phishing and pharming. Both of these methods lure users to fake websites (that appear to be legitimate), where they are asked to enter personal information. This includes login information, such as usernames and passwords, phone numbers, addresses, credit card numbers, bank account numbers, and other information criminals can use to "steal" another person's identity. For this reason, it is smart to always check the URL or Web address of a site to make sure it is legitimate before entering your personal information.

Because cybercrime covers such a broad scope of criminal activity, the examples above are only a few of the thousands of crimes that are considered cybercrimes. While computers and the Internet have made our lives easier in many ways, it is unfortunate that people also use these technologies to take advantage of others. Therefore, it is smart to protect yourself by using antivirus and spyware blocking software and being careful where you enter your personal information.

A primary impact from cybercrime is financial, and cybercrime can include many different types of profit-driven criminal activity, including ransomware attacks, email and internet fraud and identity fraud, as well as attempts to steal financial account, credit card or other payment card information. Cybercriminals may target private personal information, as well as corporate data for theft and resale.

The Council of Europe Convention on Cybercrime, to which the United States is a signatory, defines cybercrime as a wide range of malicious activities, including the illegal interception of data, system interferences that compromise network integrity and availability, and copyright infringements. Other forms of cybercrime include illegal gambling, the sale of illegal items, like weapons, drugs or counterfeit goods, as well as the solicitation, production, possession or distribution of child pornography.

The ubiquity of internet connectivity has enabled an increase in the volume and pace of cybercrime activities because the criminal no longer needs to be physically present when committing a crime. The internet's speed, convenience, anonymity and lack of borders make computer-based variations of financial crimes, such as ransomware, fraud and money laundering, as well as hate crimes, such as stalking and bullying, easier to carry out.

Cybercriminal activity may be carried out by individuals or small groups with relatively little technical skill or by highly organized global criminal groups that may include skilled developers and others with relevant expertise. To further reduce the chances of detection and prosecution, cybercriminals often choose to operate in countries with weak or nonexistent cybercrime laws.

There are many different types of cybercrime; most cybercrimes are carried out with the expectation of financial gain by the attackers, though the ways cybercriminals aim to get paid can vary. For example:

- Cyberextortion is crime involving an attack or threat of attack coupled with a demand for money to stop the attack. One form of cyberextortion is the ransomware attack, in which the attacker gains access to an organization's systems and encrypts its documents, files -- anything of potential value -- making the data inaccessible until a ransom is paid, usually in some form of cryptocurrency, such as bitcoin.
- Cryptojacking attacks use scripts to mine cryptocurrencies within browsers without the user's consent. Such attacks may

involve loading cryptocurrency mining software to the victim's system. However, many attacks depend on JavaScript code that does in-browser mining as long as the user's browser has a tab or window open on the malicious site; no malware needs to be installed as loading the affected page executes the in-browser mining code.

- Identity theft occurs when an attacker accesses a computer to glean a user's personal information that they can then use to steal that person's identity or access bank or other accounts. Cybercriminals buy and sell identity information on darknet markets, offering financial accounts, as well as other types of accounts, like video streaming services, webmail, video and audio streaming, online auctions and more. Personal health information is another frequent target of identity thieves.

- Credit card fraud occurs when hackers infiltrate retailers' systems to get the credit card and/or banking information of their customers. Stolen payment cards can be bought and sold in bulk on darknet markets, where hackers who have stolen mass quantities of credit cards profit by selling to lower-level cybercriminals who profit through credit card fraud against individual accounts.

- Ransomware is a form of cyberextortion in which the victim device is infected with malware that prevents the owner from using the device or the data stored on it. To regain access to the device or data, the victim has to pay the hacker a ransom. Ransomware can be inadvertently downloaded by opening an infected email attachment, visiting a compromised website or clicking on a pop-up ad.

- Cyberespionage occurs when a cybercriminal hacks into systems or networks to gain access to confidential information held by a government or other organization. Attacks may be motivated by profit or by ideology, and cyberespionage activities can include every type of cyberattack to gather, modify or destroy data, as well as using network-connected devices, like webcams or closed-circuit TV (CCTV) cameras, to spy on a targeted individual or groups and monitoring communications, including email, text messages and instant messages.

Impact of cybercrime on businesses

The true cost of cybercrime is difficult to accurately assess. In 2018, McAfee released a report on the economic impact of cybercrime that estimated the likely annual cost to the global economy was nearly $600 billion, up from $45 billion in 2014.

While the financial losses due to cybercrime can be significant, businesses can also suffer other disastrous consequences as a result of criminal cyberattacks, including:

- Damage to investor perception after a security breach can cause a drop in the value of a company. In addition to potential share price drops, businesses may also face increased costs for borrowing and greater difficulty in raising more capital as a result of a cyberattack.

- Loss of sensitive customer data can result in fines and penalties for companies that have failed to protect their customers' data. Businesses may also be sued over the data breach.
- Damaged brand identity and loss of reputation after a cyberattack undermine customers' trust in a company and that company's ability to keep their financial data safe. Following a cyberattack, firms not only lose current customers, they also lose the ability to gain new customers.

Businesses may also incur direct costs from a criminal cyberattack, including the cost of hiring cybersecurity companies to do incident response and remediation, as well as public relations and other services related to an attack and increased insurance premium costs.

Common types of cybercrime include online bank information theft, identity theft, online predatory crimes and unauthorized computer access. More serious crimes like cyberterrorism are also of significant concern.

Cybercrime encompasses a wide range of activities, but these can generally be broken into two categories:

- Crimes that target computer networks or devices. These types of crimes include viruses and denial-of-service (DoS) attacks.

- Crimes that use computer networks to advance other criminal activities. These types of crimes include cyberstalking, phishing and fraud or identity theft.

The FBI identifies cybercrime fugitives who have allegedly committed bank fraud and trafficked counterfeit devices that access personal electronic information. The FBI also provides information on how to report cybercrimes, as well as useful intelligence information about the latest cybercriminals.

CHAPTER TWO

EVOLUTION OF CYBERCRIME

As computer systems have now become integral to the daily functioning of businesses, organizations, governments, and individuals we have learned to put a tremendous amount of trust in these systems. As a result, we have placed incredibly important and valuable information on them. History has shown, that things of value will always be a target for a criminal. Cybercrime is no different. As people flood their personal computers, phones, and so on with valuable data, they put a target on that information for the criminal to aim for, in order to gain some form of profit from the activity.

In the past, in order for a criminal to gain access to an individual's valuables, they would have to conduct a robbery in some shape or form. In the case of data theft, the criminal would need to break into a building, sifting through files looking for the information of greatest value and profit. In our modern world, the criminal can attack their victims from a distance, and due to the nature of the internet, these acts would most likely never meet retribution.

In the 70s, we saw criminals taking advantage of the tone system used on phone networks. The attack was called phreaking, where the attacker reverse-engineered the tones used by the telephone companies to make long distance calls.

In 1988, the first computer worm made its debut on the internet and caused a great deal of destruction to organizations. This first worm was called the Morris worm, after its creator Robert Morris. While this worm was not originally intended to be malicious it still caused a great deal of damage. The U.S. Government Accountability Office in 1980 estimated that the damage could have been as high as $10,000,000.00.

1989 brought us the first known ransomware attack, which targeted the healthcare industry. Ransomware is a type of malicious software that locks a user's data, until a small ransom is paid, which will result in the issuance of a cryptographic unlock key. In this attack, an evolutionary biologist named Joseph Popp distributed 20,000 floppy disks across 90 countries, and claimed the disk contained software that could be used to analyze an individual's risk factors for contracting the AIDS virus. The disk however contained a malware program that when executed, displayed a message requiring the user to pay for a software license. Ransomware attacks have evolved greatly over the years with the healthcare field still being a very large target.

The 90s brought the web browser and email to the masses, which meant new tools for cybercriminals to exploit. This allowed the cybercriminal to greatly expand their reach. Up till this time, the cybercriminal needed to initiate a physical transaction, such as providing a floppy disk. Now cybercriminals could transmit virus code over the internet in these new, highly vulnerable web browsers. Cybercriminals took what they had learned previously and modified it to operate over the internet, with devastating results.

Cybercriminals were also able to reach out and con people from a distance with phishing attacks. No longer was it necessary to engage with individuals directly. You could attempt to trick millions of users simultaneously. Even if only a small percentage of people took the bait you stood to make a lot of money as a cybercriminal.

The 2000s brought us social media and saw the rise of identity theft. A bullseye was painted for cybercriminals with the creation of databases containing millions of users' personal identifiable information (PII), making identity theft the new financial piggy bank for criminal organizations around the world.

This information coupled with a lack of cybersecurity awareness from the general public allowed cybercriminals to commit all types of financial fraud such as opening bank accounts and credit cards in the name of others.

Every so often we experience an advance in technology that is so radical it not only changes the way that societies interact, it also has a fundamental affect on the behaviour of the criminal element within that society: introducing completely new and previously unheard of words into our everyday language usage. Henry Ford's invention of the motorcar is a classic example of this point (coining terms such as car-jacking and get-away car). Ask any criminal defense lawyer what, in their opinion, has been the most radical change in criminal behaviour, however, and probably the biggest response you'll receive is cybercrime. What, however, is cybercrime and how can it have had such a profound impact on our lives in such a short space of time?

Although you may get general consensus among criminal defense lawyers that cybercrime has been the most recent radical change in criminal behaviour, it is unlikely you'll receive the same consensus when it came to defining what cybercrime actually was. Nevertheless, broad consensus would most probably agree that cybercrime is a term of language used to describe "criminal activity that utilizes an element of a computer or computer network".

Thus, essentially there are two separate and distinct elements to cybercrime. On the one hand you have an element of exploiting weaknesses in the computer operating system or computer network. On the other hand you have an element of exploiting social fabric of a computer network, whereby a criminal makes use of the computer network to infiltrate the trust of other users of that computer network for profit or gain. Although these different elements of what constitute cybercrime may not seem overly important, they do have an impact when you look at the evolution and development of cybercrime.

Prior to the turn of the millennium large scale cybercrime centred on or around one-man operated criminals exploiting the weaknesses in the computer operating system or computer network. In most cases these crimes were committed by computer nerds who felt challenged to prove that they could beat the system. We coined the term hacker for just such a nerd, but rarely was there a financial gain element to the criminal behaviour. While a great deal of financial damage could actually result, not to mention the potential for the security risks that resulted, this one-man band criminal lacked the motive and intent of traditional criminal gangs. In short, cybercrime was infantile and largely seen as a practical joke or game by those who committed it. Criminal defense tactics at this time was also largely based on the fact that no real intentional damage was done and, in a large number of cases, the penalty for the crime was showing how the computer system had been hacked by the hacker.

Once we had all got over the fact that there was no millennium bug after all (probably the biggest cybercrime hoax of all time), cyber criminal had organized and focused their attention elsewhere. Yes, the geek element of hacking still existed – as still does today – but now hardened criminal gangs had worked out that the Internet was a safe domain, with much less risk, with which to operate and generate large profits.

In short, criminal gangs had introduced a professional element into the world of cybercrime. No longer were we looking at geeky exploitation of weaknesses in computer operating/networking systems, things had now developed to criminal gangs making use of computer networks to infiltrate and take advantage of the trust of other users of that computer network for huge financial gain.

Because of this radical change in the nature of cyber criminal activity, law makers and criminal defense lawyers began to see developments which reflected these changes. Primarily these included new cyber crimes, such as:

* Cyber-extortion – where criminal gangs threatened to close down internet-based businesses if protection money was not paid.

Worse still, threats can also be made to infiltrate the businesses security system to access financial or personal information stored therein that may then be used for financial gain

* Information theft – similar to that set-out above, only no prior approach is made to try and extort protection money and a computer network is infiltrated with the purpose of obtaining information relating to the users, whether they be an individual user of business

* Fraud – fraud has many guises on the internet, from the famous e-mails promising millions in advance fees to the sale of unmarketable quality goods. What is usually fairly consistent is an unsolicited e-mail approach by the fraudster to their victim.

* Identity theft – identity theft is where the cyber criminal steals their victims identity and then transacts, usually via the Internet in the name of the victim. More often than not this will include and element of credit card fraud.

* Exploitation of children, etc. – unfortunately many view the act of cybercrime as either harmless fun (such as hacking) or for financial gain (such as credit card fraud). However, there is also a very real and extremely nasty side to cybercrime – taking advantage of weaker members of our society. Almost weekly we now hear of cyber-criminal gangs who have been caught with child pornography.

* Intellectual property theft – strangely many computer network users do not see the illegal downloading of software and intellectual property as constituting a criminal act. In fact it is

anything but. Billions of dollars are being lost each year on illegal software and intellectual property downloads that are putting sever financial constraints on the companies that manufacture these products, many of whom are young start-ups themselves. Nevertheless, unlike other forms of cyber crimes, governments have been quick to respond to the actions of those who illegally download movies, music or software from the Internet and so, many argue, criminal defense procedures against such persons are probably the most successful and front-line of all.

* Phishing and vishing – both phishing and the more recent vishing is obtaining financial information, such as bank account records or credit card details, by sending what look like authentic messages to the recipient informing them they need to comply with certain procedures to reactivate their account. Once the information has been obtained, the criminal then defrauds the victim.

From Heartbleed and Shellshock to the Target breach and the Sony hack, cyberattacks are daily news, and yet security and compliance are often not considered as a fundamental requirement when adopting cloud computing strategies.

Cyber crime is continuously evolving as criminals identify new ways of making money from the digital revolution. However, there is no such thing as a new crime. The techniques that we see criminals use and abuse today have their antecedents in the recent past as well as antiquity. By examining the evolution of how information has been recognized as valuable, and how techniques have evolved to protect information we can better understand how techniques will need to continue to evolve to protect against the latest criminal attacks.

The widespread adoption of cloud infrastructure exposes organizations to new threats but presents new opportunities for attackers. Indeed, criminals have enthusiastically embraced the cloud as a platform for their own activities and developed "crime-as-a-service".

Data crime is more rampant than ever, and every SMB should have a disaster recovery plan (DRP) that anticipates the possibility of data corruption or worse. Like criminals who progress from breaking and entering, to grand theft auto, to abduction, ransom and capital crimes, data hackers and terrorists are stalking the livelihood of businesses worldwide.

From simple beginnings of starting fires or stealing files, data criminals have become more sophisticated to the point of studying the latest cybersecurity techniques and devising ways to subvert them. History has taught us that total prevention may be elusive. As data storage, retrieval and applications have become more modernized and data made more accessible, the downside is that this accessibility creates more opportunities for misuse.

Cybercrime had its beginnings in simpler times, when data theft was a military strategy. Information has always meant power.

Data theft is as old as civilization itself. Every empire had spies to uncover secrets of opposing regimes. Egypt, for example, was constantly seeking information on the political and military strength of Greece and Rome, while it was said that Moses used spies to gain information on surrounding towns for food and military advantages. Alan Turing led a team of code-breakers to decipher German U-Boat codes to help turn the tide in World War II. Wartime espionage has existed in every time period.

Data theft has even become a focal point in popular movies. The Imitation Game depicts Alan Turing's achievements mentioned above, while another movie, It's a Wonderful Life, shows how the theft of bank assets can lead to business foreclosure and personal despair. Disaster recovery, in this case, depended on the charity of local townspeople.

But most businesses don't have town benefactors and must rely on their own form of protection. In the 1970s, digital technology became available, and IT departments were asked to support the exchange of data through electronic media like tape and disk. The promise of technology was tainted by the dangers of losing it and the often dire consequences of down time. SMBs began to plan for such emergencies and the idea of data and resource backup became more prevalent – the beginnings of disaster recovery planning.

In The Life of Reason, the philosopher George Santayana wrote, "Those who cannot remember the past are condemned to repeat it." It is wise for SMBs to remember the past and prepare for the future because disasters are not only naturally occurring but also being constantly planned in the minds of cyber criminals.

Insider theft and malware should be high on the list of concerns for IT security executives. Cybercrime technology keeps evolving, and SMBs need to keep pace by evolving prevention and recovery strategies. This includes management awareness, budgeting, organizational training, and improving technology – in particular, better use of firewalls and encryption.

Fraud, data leaks, malware/ransomware and terrorist attacks can be just as damaging as natural disasters. Ransomware is a type of malware that encrypts or locks files on a computer or server and then demands payment to have the files unlocked. The cybercriminal may or may not provide the unlocking key after payment and may, in fact, escalate the situation by asking for increasingly higher payments. The best forms of protection are data backup and anti-virus software.

There are many types of ransomware, including Cryptolocker, Locky, Telacrypt, and Cryptowall. Cryptolocker has been around since 2013. Spread through email attachments, it encrypts certain kinds of files on local and network-mounted drives. It then displays the "ransom message" asking for payment to unlock the files. Cryptowall is a variant of Cryptolocker and is thought to have originated in Australia in 2014.

Denial of Service (DoS) is a type of malware that tries to make resources unavailable to intended users, like interrupting connection to the Internet. If there are multiple attack sources, it is called Distributed Denial of Service (DDoS). These attacks are typically aimed at financial institutions, banks and credit card processors.

The National Fraud Centre, Inc. reports cybercrime is becoming rapidly more sophisticated, with underground websites being developed to receive and re-sell sensitive information to facilitate the distribution of stolen data.

Cybercrime invades all countries and all industries. Call center data leaks and fraud have been reported from India to Scotland. As reported in The Economic Times, a vendor survey was recently conducted of 208 C-level security and IT professionals across different geographies and sectors in India. The survey reveals that 69 percent of respondents "experienced an attempted or realised data theft or corruption by corporate insiders over the past 12 months."

In the UK, meanwhile, the National Crime Agency (NCA) has published its "Cyber Crime Assessment 2016," outlining current threats to UK businesses. The assessment states that cybercrime is increasing in the UK, fuelled by significant increases in distributed denial of service (DDoS) and ransomware attacks. The most common crime against businesses is breach of data, with the annual cost to the UK estimated in the billions of pounds. The NCA encourages companies to view cybercrime as a board-level issue, not just a technical one. Crime prevention and disaster recovery planning should have a top priority with all businesses.

As reported by RT news, a US spokesperson has said America is "in the midst of a revolution of the cyber threat." White House counterterrorism advisor Lisa Monaco compared cyber-attacks to cases of terrorism and said that the White House is launching new sanctions for "significant cyber incidents." Several federal agencies are being tasked with dealing with cybercrime and its aftermath, including the FBI and Homeland Security departments.

Ransomware attacks in both the US and UK have had more impact than executives expected. Research conducted by Merrill Research (2016 Executive Application & Network Security Survey) revealed that 84 percent of US and UK IT executives said they would never pay a ransom for a cyberattack. And yet, of those companies who were actually attacked, 43 percent said they did exactly that.

In Australia, the government has developed a national cyber security strategy, listing 33 initiatives to fight cybercrime supported by a budget of $230 million; in Hamburg, the Chaos Computer Club looks for flaws in government IT systems; in the Netherlands, it's the Europol Internet Crime unit that watches online activity.

Tom Kellermann, a noted consultant on cybersecurity, has said, "East Europeans are master craftsmen when it comes to malware development. East European malware are so elegantly crafted, they have been dubbed the Faberge Eggs of the malware world."

The Radware research, reported on continuitycentral.com, suggests that future cyber threats will be aimed at category devices like wearables and the Internet of Things (IoT). Executives fear losses to their business will be felt in many ways including reputation, operations, productivity, revenue, and share price value.

These are universal issues affecting every SMB worldwide, irrespective of location or proximity to a potential natural disaster.

McAffee and the Centre for Strategic and International Studies (CSIC) studied the impact of cybercrime. Their conclusion is that "cybercrime is a growth industry." They estimated that in 2014 the likely annual cost to the global economy from cybercrime was more than $400 billion – exceeding the national income of most countries and governments in the world.

A recent study conducted by the Ponemon Institute and sponsored by IBM showed that the average cost of a data breach for companies surveyed was $4 million – a 29 percent increase since 2013. The highest cost per record lost was $355, in the healthcare industry.

There have been many recent examples of data theft from large organizations that show the serious business impact of criminal activity.

In 2006, for example, a US Department of Veterans Affairs employee took his laptop home. The information on that laptop was stolen, with the names, birthdates, and social security numbers of 17.5 million military veterans and personnel. The VA was forced to staff a call centre, send out millions of mailings, and pay for credit monitoring for victims. According to the Ponemon Institute, the estimated cost of the breach has been $25 million.

In another example, in 2011, hackers stole millions of names and email addresses from Epsilon, a Dallas-based marketing firm that handles ecommerce for companies like Best Buy and JP Morgan. It is estimated that the lost customer base and eventual misuse of stolen data will cost somewhere between $100 million and $2-4 billion.

More recently, Sony Corporation exposed the data of more than 100 million customer accounts on its PlayStation and Sony Online Entertainment networks. The estimated loss from this breach is $2 billion.

If breaches can happen to large enterprises like these, it is even more likely that they can happen to SMBs. Let history be our teacher.

Cybercrime is becoming woven into the fabric of worldwide commerce. It comes in many forms, is perpetrated by amateurs and professionals, insiders and outsiders, in every developed country. It costs private companies, public companies, and governments hundreds of millions of dollars every year, and such organizations need to better recognize the true existential threat that it presents. Continual vigilance is needed to watch not only data movement, but unusual behaviour and questionable relationships. Behind every cybercrime is a cybercriminal.

CHAPTER THREE

A LEGAL PERSPECTIVE OF CYBERCRIME

In 2011, at least 2.3 billion people, the equivalent of more than one third of the world's total population, had access to the internet. Over 60 per cent of all internet users are in developing countries, with 45 per cent of all internet users below the age of 25 years. By the year 2017, it is estimated that mobile broadband subscriptions will approach 70 per cent of the world's total population. By the year 2020, the number of networked devices (the 'internet of things') will outnumber people by six to one, transforming current conceptions of the internet. In the hyperconnected world of tomorrow, it will become hard to imagine a 'computer crime', and perhaps any crime, that does not involve electronic evidence linked with internet protocol (IP) connectivity.

'Definitions' of cybercrime mostly depend upon the purpose of using the term. A limited number of acts against the confidentiality, integrity and availability of computer data or systems represent the core of cybercrime. Beyond this, however, computer-related acts for personal or financial gain or harm, including forms of identity-related crime, and computer content-related acts (all of which fall within a wider meaning of the term 'cybercrime') do not lend themselves easily to efforts to arrive at legal definitions of the aggregate term. Certain definitions are required for the core of cybercrime acts. However, a 'definition' of cybercrime is not as relevant for other purposes, such as defining the scope of specialized investigative and international cooperation powers, which are better focused on electronic evidence for any crime, rather than a broad, artificial 'cybercrime' construct.

In many countries, the explosion in global connectivity has come at a time of economic and demographic transformations, with rising income disparities, tightened private sector spending, and reduced financial liquidity. At the global level, law enforcement respondents to the study perceive increasing levels of cybercrime, as both individuals and organized criminal groups exploit new criminal opportunities, driven by profit and personal gain. Upwards of 80 per cent of cybercrime acts are estimated to originate in some form of organized activity, with cybercrime black markets established on a cycle of malware creation, computer infection, botnet management, harvesting of personal and financial data, data sale, and 'cashing out' of financial information.

Cybercrime perpetrators no longer require complex skills or techniques. In the developing country context in particular, subcultures of young men engaged in computer-related financial fraud have emerged, many of whom begin involvement in cybercrime in late teenage years. Globally, cybercrime acts show a broad distribution across financial-driven acts, and computer-content related acts, as well as acts against the confidentiality, integrity and accessibility of computer systems. Perceptions of relative risk and threat vary, however, between Governments and private sector enterprises. Currently, police-recorded crime statistics do not represent a sound basis for cross-national comparisons, although such statistics are often important for policy making at the national level.

Two-thirds of countries view their systems of police statistics as insufficient for recording cybercrime. Police-recorded cybercrime rates are associated with levels of country development and specialized police capacity, rather than underlying crime rates.

Victimization surveys represent a more sound basis for comparison. These demonstrate that individual cybercrime victimization is significantly higher than for 'conventional' crime forms. Victimization rates for online credit card fraud, identity theft, responding to a phishing attempt, and experiencing unauthorized access to an email account, vary between 1 and 17 per cent of the online population for 21 countries across the world, compared with typical burglary, robbery and car theft rates of under 5 per cent for these same countries. Cybercrime victimization rates are higher in countries with lower levels of development, highlighting a need to strengthen prevention efforts in these countries.

Private sector enterprises in Europe report similar victimization rates – between 2 and 16 per cent – for acts such as data breach due to intrusion or phishing. Criminal tools of choice for these crimes, such as botnets, have global reach. More than one million unique IP addresses globally functioned as botnet command and control servers in 2011. Internet content also represented a significant concern for Governments. Material targeted for removal includes child pornography and hate speech, but also content related to defamation and government criticism, raising human rights law concerns in some cases. Almost 24 per cent of total global internet traffic is estimated to infringe copyright, with downloads of shared peer-to-peer (P2P) material particularly high in countries in Africa, South America, and Western and South Asia.

Legal measures play a key role in the prevention and combating of cybercrime. These are required in all areas, including criminalization, procedural powers, jurisdiction, international cooperation, and internet service provider responsibility and liability. At the national level, both existing and new (or planned), cybercrime laws most often concern criminalization, indicating a predominant focus on establishing specialized offences for core cybercrime acts. Countries increasingly recognize, however, the need for legislation in other areas.

Compared to existing laws, new or planned cybercrime laws more frequently address investigative measures, jurisdiction, electronic evidence and international cooperation. Globally, less than half of responding countries perceive their criminal and procedural law frameworks to be sufficient, although this masks large regional differences. While more than two-thirds of countries in Europe report sufficient legislation, the picture is reversed in Africa, the Americas, Asia and Oceania, where more than two-thirds of countries view laws as only partly sufficient, or not sufficient at all. Only one half of the countries, which reported that laws were insufficient, also indicated new or planned laws, thus highlighting an urgent need for legislative strengthening in these regions.

The last decade has seen significant developments in the promulgation of international and regional instruments aimed at countering cybercrime. These include binding and non-binding instruments. Five clusters can be identified, consisting of instruments developed in the context of, or inspired by: (i) the Council of Europe or the European Union, (ii) the Commonwealth of Independent States or the Shanghai Cooperation Organization, (iii) intergovernmental

African organizations, (iv) the League of Arab States, and (v) the United Nations. A significant amount of cross-fertilization exists between all instruments, including, in particular, concepts and approaches developed in the Council of Europe Convention on Cybercrime. Analysis of the articles of 19 multilateral instruments relevant to cybercrime shows common core provisions, but also significant divergence in substantive areas addressed.

Globally, 82 countries have signed and/or ratified a binding cybercrime instrument. In addition to formal membership and implementation, multilateral cybercrime instruments have influenced national laws indirectly, through use as a model by non-States parties, or via the influence of legislation of States parties on other countries. Membership of a multilateral cybercrime instrument corresponds with the perception of increased sufficiency of national criminal and procedural law, indicating that current multilateral provisions in these areas are generally considered effective.

For the more than 40 countries that provided information, the Council of Europe Convention on Cybercrime is the most used multilateral instrument for the development of cybercrime legislation. Altogether, multilateral instruments from other 'clusters' were used in around half as many countries.

Overall, one-third of responding countries report that their legislation is highly, or very highly, harmonized with countries viewed as important for the purposes of international cooperation. This varies regionally, however, with higher degrees of harmonization reported within the Americas and Europe. This may be due to the use, in some regions, of multilateral instruments, which are inherently designed to play a role in harmonization. Fragmentation at the international level, and diversity of national laws, in terms of cybercrime acts criminalized, jurisdictional bases, and mechanisms of cooperation, may correlate with the existence of multiple cybercrime instruments with different thematic and geographic scope. Both instruments and regions presently reflect divergences derived from underlying legal and constitutional differences, including differing conceptions of rights and privacy.

Information on cybercrime criminal laws was gathered through the study questionnaire, as well as by primary source analysis of available legislation collected by the Secretariat. The study questionnaire referred to 14 acts commonly included in notions of cybercrime. Responding countries described widespread criminalization of these 14 acts, with the primary exception of SPAM offences and, to some extent, offences concerning computer misuse tools, racism and xenophobia, and online solicitation or 'grooming' of children.

This reflects a certain baseline consensus on culpable cybercrime conduct. Countries reported few additional crimes, not mentioned in the questionnaire. These mostly concerned computer content, including criminalization of obscene material, online gambling, and online illicit markets, such as in drugs and persons. For the 14 acts, countries reported the use of cyber-specific offences for core cybercrime acts against the confidentiality, integrity and accessibility of computer systems. For other forms of cybercrime, general (non-cyber-specific) offences were used more often. Both approaches were reported, however, for computer-related acts involving breach of privacy, fraud or forgery, and identity offences.

While high-level consensus exists regarding broad areas of criminalization, detailed analysis of the provisions in source legislation reveals divergent approaches. Offences involving illegal access to computer systems and data differ with respect to the object of the offence (data, system, or information), and regarding the criminalization of 'mere' access or the requirement for further intent, such as to cause loss or damage. The requisite intent for an offence also differs in approaches to criminalization of interference with computer systems or data. Most countries require the interference to be intentional, while others include reckless interference. For interference with computer data, the conduct constituting interference ranges from damaging or deleting, to altering, suppressing, inputting or transmitting data.

Criminalization of illegal interception differs by virtue of whether the offence is restricted to non-public data transmissions or not, and concerning whether the crime is restricted to interception 'by technical means'. Not all countries criminalize computer misuse tools. For those that do, differences arise regarding whether the offence covers possession, dissemination, or use of software (such as malware) and/or computer access codes (such as victim passwords). From the perspective of international cooperation, such differences may have an impact upon findings of dual-criminality between countries.

Several countries have adopted cyber-specific crimes for computer-related fraud, forgery and identity offences. Others extend general provisions on fraud or theft, or rely on crimes covering constituent elements – such as illegal access, data interference and forgery, in the case of identity offences. A number of content-related offences, particularly those concerning child pornography, show widespread criminalization. Differences arise however regarding the definition of 'child', limitations in relation to 'visual' material or exclusion of simulated material, and acts covered. Although the vast majority of countries, for instance, cover production and distribution of child pornography, criminalization of possession and access shows greater variation. For computer-related copyright and trademark infringement, countries most usually reported the application of general criminal offences for acts committed willfully and on a commercial scale.

The increasing use of social media and user-generated internet content has resulted in regulatory responses from governments, including the use of criminal law, and calls for respect for rights to freedom of expression. Responding countries report varying boundaries to expression, including with respect to defamation, contempt, threats, incitement to hatred, insult to religious feelings, obscene material, and undermining the state. The socio-cultural element of some limitations is reflected not only in national law, but also in multilateral instruments. Some regional cybercrime instruments, for example, contain broad offences regarding the violation of public morals, pornographic material, and religious or family principles or values.

International human rights law acts both as a sword and a shield, requiring criminalization of (limited) extreme forms of expression, while protecting other forms. Some prohibitions on freedom of expression, including incitement to genocide, hatred constituting incitement to discrimination, hostility or violence, incitement to terrorism, and propaganda for war, are therefore required for States that are party to relevant international human rights instruments. For others, the 'margin of appreciation' allows leeway to countries in determining the boundaries of acceptable expression in line with their own cultures and legal traditions. Nonetheless, international human rights law will intervene at a certain point. Penal laws on defamation, disrespect for authority, and insult, for example, that apply to online expressions will face a high threshold of demonstrating that the measures are proportionate, appropriate, and the least intrusive possible. Where content is illegal in one country, but legal to produce and disseminate in another, States will need to focus criminal justice responses on persons accessing content within the national jurisdiction, rather than on content produced outside of the country.

Over 90 per cent of responding countries report that cybercrime acts most frequently come to the attention of law enforcement authorities through reports by individual or corporate victims. Responding countries estimate that the proportion of actual cybercrime victimization reported to the police ranges upwards from 1 per cent. One global private sector survey suggests that 80 per cent of individual victims of core cybercrime do not report the crime to the police. Underreporting derives from a lack of awareness of victimization and of reporting mechanisms, victim shame and embarrassment, and perceived reputation risks for corporations. Authorities in all regions of the world highlighted initiatives for increasing reporting, including online and hotline reporting systems, public awareness campaigns, private sector liaison, and enhanced police outreach and information sharing. An incident-driven response to cybercrime must, however, be accompanied by medium and long-term tactical investigations that focus on crime markets and criminal scheme architects. Law enforcement authorities in developed countries are engaged in this area, including through undercover units targeting offenders on social networking sites, chat rooms, and instant messaging and P2P services. Challenges in the investigation of cybercrime arise from criminal innovations by offenders, difficulties in accessing electronic evidence, and from internal resource, capacity and logistical limitations. Suspects frequently use anonymization and obfuscation technologies, and new techniques quickly make their way to a broad criminal audience through online crime markets.

Law enforcement cybercrime investigations require an amalgamation of traditional and new policing techniques. While some investigative actions can be achieved with traditional powers, many procedural provisions do not translate well from a spatial, object-oriented approach to one involving electronic data storage and real-time data flows. The study questionnaire referred to ten cybercrime investigative measures, ranging from generic search and seizure to specialized powers, such as preservation of computer data. Countries most often reported the existence of general (noncyber-specific) powers across all investigative measures. A number of countries also reported cyber-specific legislation, notably for ensuring expedited preservation of computer data and obtaining stored subscriber data.

Many countries reported a lack of legal power for advanced measures, such as remote computer forensics. While traditional procedural powers can be extended to cybersituations, in many cases such an approach can also lead to legal uncertainties and challenges to the lawfulness of evidence gathering, and thus the admissibility of evidence. Overall, national approaches to cybercrime investigative powers show less core commonality than for criminalization of many cybercrime acts.

Irrespective of the legal form of investigative powers, all responding authorities use search and seizure for the physical appropriation of computer equipment and the capture of computer data. The majority of countries also use orders for obtaining stored computer data from internet service providers. Outside of Europe, however, around one third of countries report challenges in compelling third parties in an investigation to provide information. Around three-quarters of countries use specialized investigative measures, such as real-time collection of data, or expedited preservation of data. Use of investigative measures typically requires a minimum of initial evidence or a report of a cybercrime act. More intrusive measures, such as those involving real-time collection of data or accessing of data content, often require higher thresholds, such as evidence of a serious act, or demonstration of probable cause or reasonable grounds.

The interplay between law enforcement and internet service providers is particularly complex. Service providers hold subscriber information, billing invoices, some connection logs, location information (such as cell tower data for mobile providers), and communication content, all of which can represent critical electronic evidence of an offence. National legal obligations and private sector data retention and disclosure policies vary widely by country, industry and type of data. Countries most often reported using court orders to obtain evidence from service providers. In some cases, however, law enforcement may be able to obtain stored subscriber data, traffic data, and even content data, directly. In this respect, private sector organizations often reported both a primary policy of requiring due legal process for data disclosure, but also voluntary compliance with direct law enforcement requests under some circumstances. Informal relationships between law enforcement and service providers, the existence of which was reported in more than half of all responding countries, assist the process of information exchange and trust-building. Responses indicated that there is a need to balance privacy and due process, with disclosure of evidence in a timely manner, in order to ensure that the private sector does not become a 'choke-point' for investigations.

Cybercrime investigations invariably involve considerations of privacy under international human rights law. Human rights standards specify that laws must be sufficiently clear to give an adequate indication of the circumstances in which authorities are empowered to use an investigative measure, and that adequate and effective guarantees must exist against abuse. Countries reported the protection of privacy rights in national law, as well as a range of limits and safeguards on investigations. When investigations are transnational, divergences in levels of protection, however, give rise to unpredictability regarding foreign law enforcement access to data, and potential jurisdictional gaps in privacy protection regimes.

Over 90 per cent of the countries that responded to the questionnaire have begun to put in place specialized structures for the investigation of cybercrime and crimes involving electronic evidence. In developing countries, however, these are not well resourced and suffer from a capacity shortage. Countries with lower levels of development have significantly fewer specialized police, with around 0.2 per 100,000 national internet users. The rate is two to five times higher in more developed countries. Seventy per cent of specialized law enforcement officers in less developed countries were reported to lack computer skills and equipment, and only half receive training more than once a year.

More than half of responding countries in Africa, and one-third of countries in the Americas report that law enforcement resources for investigating cybercrime were insufficient. Globally, it is likely that the picture is worse. The study received responses, for example, from only 20 per cent of the world's 50 least developed countries.

All responding countries in Africa, and over 80 per cent of countries in the Americas and Asia and Oceania reported requiring technical assistance. The most commonly cited area for technical assistance required was general cybercrime investigative techniques. Of those countries requiring assistance, 60 per cent indicated that this was needed by law enforcement agencies.

Evidence is the means by which facts relevant to the guilt or innocence of an individual at trial are established. Electronic evidence is all such material that exists in electronic, or digital, form. It can be stored or transient. It can exist in the form of computer files, transmissions, logs, metadata, or network data. Digital forensics is concerned with recovering – often volatile and easily contaminated – information that may have evidential value. Forensics techniques include the creation of 'bit-for-bit' copies of stored and deleted information, 'writeblocking' in order to ensure that the original information is not changed, and cryptographic file 'hashes', or digital signatures, that can demonstrate changes in information. Almost all countries reported some digital forensics capacity. Many responding countries, across all regions, however, note insufficient numbers of forensic examiners, differences between capacity at federal and state level, lack of forensics tools, and backlogs due to overwhelming quantities of data for analysis. One half of countries report that suspects make use of encryption, rendering access to this type of evidence difficult and time-consuming without the decryption key. In most countries, the task of analyzing electronic evidence lies with law enforcement authorities.

Prosecutors, however, must view and understand electronic evidence in order to build a case at trial. All countries in Africa and one-third of countries in other regions reported insufficient resources for prosecutors to do so. Prosecution computer skills are typically lower than those of investigators. Globally, around 65 per cent of responding countries report some form of prosecutorial cybercrime specialization. Just 10 per cent of countries report specialized judicial services. The vast majority of cybercrime cases are handled by non-specialized judges, who, in 40 per cent of responding countries, do not receive any form of cybercrime-related training. Judicial training on cybercrime law, evidence collection, and basic and advanced computer knowledge represents a particular priority.

Over 60 per cent of responding countries do not make a legal distinction between electronic evidence and physical evidence. While approaches vary, many countries consider this good practice, as it ensures fair admissibility alongside all other types of evidence. A number of countries outside of Europe do not admit electronic evidence at all, making the prosecution of cybercrime, and any other crime evidenced by electronic information, unfeasible. While countries do not, in general, have separate evidentiary rules for electronic evidence, a number of countries referred to principles such as: the best evidence rule, the relevance of evidence, the hearsay rule, authenticity, and integrity, all of which may have particular application to electronic evidence. Many countries highlighted challenges of attribution of acts to a particular individual, and commented that this was often dependent upon circumstantial evidence.

The challenges facing both law enforcement investigators and prosecutors mean that 'brought to justice' rates are low for cybercrime offenders. Suspects identified per police recorded offence are comparable for child pornography offences to other sex offences. However, suspects per recorded offence for acts such as illegal access and computer-related fraud or forgery are only around 25 per 100 offences. Very few countries were able to provide data on persons prosecuted or convicted. Calculations for cybercrime offences in one country, however, show that the ratio of persons convicted to recorded offences, is significantly lower than for other 'conventional' crimes.

Countries responding to the study questionnaire report that between 30 and 70 per cent of cybercrime acts involve a transnational dimension, engaging issues of transnational investigations, sovereignty, jurisdiction, extraterritorial evidence, and a requirement for international cooperation. A transnational dimension to a cybercrime offence arises where an element or substantial effect of the offence is in another territory, or where part of the modus operandi of the offence is in another territory. International law provides for a number of bases of jurisdiction over such acts, including forms of territory-based jurisdiction and nationality based jurisdiction.

Some of these bases are also found in multilateral cybercrime instruments. While all countries in Europe consider that national laws provide a sufficient framework for the criminalization and prosecution of extraterritorial cybercrime acts, around one-third to over one-half of countries in other regions of the world report insufficient frameworks. In many countries, provisions reflect the idea that the 'whole' offence need not take place within the country in order to assert territorial jurisdiction.

Territorial linkages can be made with reference to elements or effects of the act, or the location of computer systems or data utilized for the offence. Where they arise, jurisdictional conflicts are typically resolved through formal and informal consultations between countries. Country responses do not reveal, at present, any need for additional forms of jurisdiction over a putative 'cyberspace' dimension. Rather, forms of territoriality-based and nationality-based jurisdiction are almost always able to ensure a sufficient connection between cybercrime acts and at least one State.

Forms of international cooperation include extradition, mutual legal assistance, mutual recognition of foreign judgments, and informal policeto-police cooperation. Due to the volatile nature of electronic evidence, international cooperation in criminal matters in the area of cybercrime requires timely responses and the ability to request specialized investigative actions, such as preservation of computer data.

Use of traditional forms of cooperation predominates for obtaining extra-territorial evidence in cybercrime cases, with over 70 per cent of countries reporting using formal mutual legal assistance requests for this purpose. Within such formal cooperation, almost 60 per cent of requests use bilateral instruments as the legal basis. Multilateral instruments are used in 20 per cent of cases. Response times for formal mechanisms were reported to be of the order of months, for extradition and mutual legal assistance requests, a timescale which presents challenges to the collection of volatile electronic evidence.

Sixty per cent of countries in Africa, the Americas and Europe, and 20 per cent in Asia and Oceania, report channels for urgent requests. However, the impact of these on response times is unclear. Modes of informal cooperation are possible for around two-thirds of reporting countries, although few countries have a policy for the use of such mechanisms. Initiatives for informal cooperation and for facilitating formal cooperation, such as 24/7 networks, offer important potential for faster response times. They are, however, under-utilized, handling around three per cent of the total number of cybercrime cases encountered by law enforcement for the group of reporting countries.

Formal and informal modes of cooperation are designed to manage the process of State consent for the conduct of foreign law enforcement investigations that affect a State's sovereignty. Increasingly, however, investigators, knowingly or unknowingly, access extraterritorial data during evidence gathering, without the consent of the State where the data is physically situated. This situation arises, in particular, due to cloud computing technologies which involve data storage at multiple data centres in different geographic locations. Data 'location', whilst technically knowable, is becoming increasingly artificial, to the extent that even traditional mutual legal assistance requests will often be addressed to the country that is the seat of the service provider, rather than the country where the data centre is physically located.

Direct foreign law enforcement access to extraterritorial data could occur when investigators make use of an existing live connection from a suspect's device, or where investigators use lawfully obtained data access credentials. Law enforcement investigators may, on occasion, obtain data from extra-territorial service providers through an informal direct request, although service providers usually require due legal process. Relevant existing provisions on 'trans-border' access found in the Council of Europe Cybercrime Convention and the League of Arab States Convention on Information Technology Offences do not adequately cover such situations, due to a focus on the 'consent' of the person having lawful authority to disclose the data, and presumed knowledge of the location of the data at the time of access or receipt.

The current international cooperation picture risks the emergence of country clusters that have the necessary powers and procedures to cooperate amongst themselves, but are restricted, for all other countries, to 'traditional' modes of international cooperation that take no account of the specificities of electronic evidence and the global nature of cybercrime.

This is particularly the case for cooperation in investigative actions. A lack of common approach, including within current multilateral cybercrime instruments, means that requests for actions, such as expedited preservation of data outside of those countries with international obligations to ensure such a facility and to make it available upon request, may not be easily fulfilled. The inclusion of this power in the draft African Union Cybersecurity Convention may go some way towards closing this lacuna.

Globally, divergences in the scope of cooperation provisions in multilateral and bilateral instruments, a lack of response time obligation, a lack of agreement on permissible direct access to extraterritorial data, multiple informal law enforcement networks, and variance in cooperation safeguards, represent significant challenges to effective international cooperation regarding electronic evidence in criminal matters.

Crime prevention comprises strategies and measures that seek to reduce the risk of crimes occurring, and mitigate potential harmful effects on individuals and society. Almost 40 per cent of responding countries report the existence of national law or policy on cybercrime prevention. Initiatives are under preparation in a further 20 per cent of countries. Countries highlight that good practices on cybercrime prevention include the promulgation of legislation, effective leadership, development of criminal justice and law enforcement capacity, education and awareness, the development of a strong knowledge base, and cooperation across government, communities, the private sector and internationally.

More than one half of countries report the existence of cybercrime strategies. In many cases, cybercrime strategies are closely integrated in cybersecurity strategies. Around 70 per cent of all countries reported national strategies included components on awareness raising, international cooperation, and law enforcement capacity. For the purposes of coordination, law enforcement and prosecution agencies are most frequently reported as lead cybercrime institutions.

Surveys, including in developing countries, demonstrate that most individual internet users now take basic security precautions. The continued importance of public awareness raising campaigns, including those covering emerging threats, and those targeted at specific audiences, such as children, was highlighted by responding Governments, private sector entities, and academic institutions. User education is most effective when combined with systems that help users to achieve their goals in a secure manner.

If user cost is higher than direct user benefit, individuals have little incentive to follow security measures. Private sector entities also report that user and employee awareness must be integrated into a holistic approach to security. Foundational principles and good practice referred to include accountability for acting on awareness, risk management policies and practices, board-level leadership, and staff training.

Two-thirds of private sector respondents had conducted a cybercrime risk assessment, and most reported use of cybersecurity technology such as firewalls, digital evidence preservation, content identification, intrusion detection, and system supervision and monitoring. Concern was expressed, however, that small and medium-sized companies either do not take sufficient steps to protect systems, or incorrectly perceive that they will not be a target.

Regulatory frameworks have an important role to play in cybercrime prevention, both with respect to the private sector in general and service providers in particular. Nearly half of countries have passed data protection laws, which specify requirements for the protection and use of personal data. Some of these regimes include specific requirements for internet service providers and other electronic communications providers. While data protection laws require personal data to be deleted when no longer required, some countries have made exceptions for the purposes of criminal investigations, requiring internet service providers to store specific types of data for a period of time.

Many developed countries also have rules requiring organizations to notify individuals and regulators of data breaches. Internet service providers typically have limited liability as 'mere conduits' of data. Modification of transmitted content increases liability, as does actual or constructive knowledge of an illegal activity. Expeditious action after notification, on the other hand, reduces liability. While technical possibilities exist for filtering of internet content by service providers, restrictions on internet access are subject to foreseeability and proportionality requirements under international human rights law protecting rights to seek, receive and impart information.

Public-private partnerships are central to cybercrime prevention. Over half of all countries report the existence of partnerships. These are created in equal numbers by informal agreement and by legal basis. Private sector entities are most often involved in partnerships, followed by academic institutions, and international and regional organizations. Partnerships are mostly used for facilitating the exchange of information on threats and trends, but also for prevention activities, and action in specific cases. Within the context of some public-private partnerships, private sector entities have taken proactive approaches to investigating and taking legal action against cybercrime operations. Such actions complement those of law enforcement and can help mitigate damage to victims. Academic institutions play a variety of roles in preventing cybercrime, including through delivery of education and training to professionals, law and policy development, and work on technical standards and solution development. Universities house and facilitate cybercrime experts, some computer emergency response teams (CERTs), and specialized research centres.

CHAPTER FOUR
INTERNATIONAL INSTRUMENTS FOR COMBATING CYBERCRIME

Cybercrime is a new range of international law, particularly international criminal law. The existence of cybercrime is now a fact that should be taken seriously by the international community. It creates then intersection with other crimes such as crime of aggression and other crimes. Immediate response form is needed to regulate cybercrime internationally because the fact shows that no one convention has found cybercrime internationally. The existed Convention of Cyber Crime enacts only regionally like European Convention of Cyber Crime.

The needs of international law instrument are the basic need of international community to handle cybercrime and its intersection to other crimes including crime of aggression. Until now, there is no international law treaty concerning cybercrime. Some current cybercrime regulations are enacted regionally and domestically. Those regulation can be assumed as a part of cyber security system to protect every individual both active and passive user.

As computers have developed, so have also criminal offences associated with their use. Mankind will always have to live with criminal activity and as a result of the conversion to the use of computer networks in the online society on cyberspace, new methods of perpetrating crimes have been developed. Now-a-days new high-tech forms of crimes are committed which include phishing, Botnet attacks, piracy, malicious spreading of virus, attacks of criminal groups on critical information infrastructure and hacking. So, we can say that crime and punishment are largely local, regional or national. Today many differences confronting us are associated with the transnational character of cybercrimes. It is therefore, important to have international legal instruments ready to serve anti-crime efforts.

The international legal instruments for preventing the criminal activities in cyberspace include:

European Convention on Cybercrime (ECC)
The Convention came into effect on June 2001 with the purpose to pursue a common criminal policy against cybercrime. Along with the Council of Europe the Convention was signed by US, Canada and Japan. It is one of the first international treaties on crimes committed using internet or other computer networks. It has three main aims which include:
- To harmonize substantive laws
- To align procedural laws
- and to implement an effective system of international co-operation

However, its main focus is to deal with infringements of copyright, child pornography, computer related fraud and violations of network security. And such problems are dealt by Convention by providing the common perception on cybercrimes, authentication of cyber-crime acts, jurisdiction and international co-operation in dealing with it.

The Convention contains four chapters in all:

First Chapter - deals with definitions like computer system, computer data, service provider and traffic data.

Second Chapter - focuses on the measures that are to be taken by the signing nations at National level. And, these measures relate to substantive criminal law, procedural law and Jurisdiction.

Third Chapter - makes mandatory for nations to cooperate with each other to deal effectively with the cybercrimes.

Fourth Chapter - provides for signature by the parties to the convention.

The only binding international instrument against cybercrime nowadays is ECC. It serves as a guideline for any country developing comprehensive national legislation against cybercrime and as a framework for international cooperation between state parties. It has been also ratified and accessed by 41 countries and 11 countries signed without following with ratification. It has been entry into force on 1 July 2004.

It covers type of cybercrime such as illegal access, illegal interception, data and system interference, misuse of devices, computer-related forgery, computer-related fraud, offences related to child pornography, offences related to infringements of copyright and related rights (article 2-11 of ECC).

Computer crimes present unique problems due to the global nature of the Internet. On the Internet, where borders are meaningless, we are vulnerable to criminals from all over the world. The Internet's disregard of national borders poses significant difficulties for law enforcement officials who must operate within national borders while attempting to prosecute computer crimes.

It is apparent that an adequate global uniformity cannot be achieved in national laws because computer crime laws are still lacking in many countries in Africa and Asia. Many developing countries lack the necessary technical infrastructure and subsequent computer use among their populations. Computer crime simply cannot be an priority issue because it is not considered a problem or even a potential problem particularly in those countries. It sometimes may be beneficial for a nation to become a computer crime haven. For example, many of the former Soviet Republics are already major de facto computer crime havens.

Criminals may capture the political process with threats or bribes, making the local national government unable to pass the appropriate legislation. A country may also choose to become a computer crime haven in order to secure large aid awards from the United States and other industrialized nations. A nation with such aims could hope to receive millions in aid to wage a war on computer crime.

Cyberspace makes physical location irrelevant. It is as easy to victimize someone who is halfway around the world as it is your next-door neighbor. There is currently no effective way to police cyberspace because our experience with computer crime is still very low. Given the nature of the cyberspace, computer crime requires developing a new model of law enforcement.

The nature of computer crime makes it too difficult for law enforcement to effectively combat the problem. The traditional model of law enforcement is not an effective strategy for dealing with computer crime. While "cybercrime" alters assumptions about the relationship between internal order and external threats, it is important to examine the computer crimes and international approaches to computer crime enforcement.

In general, "computer crime" is a crime where a computer system itself is the target. Computer crime can be defined as any violation of criminal law that involves knowledge of computer technology for its perpetration, investigation, or prosecution. Because of the diversity of computer-related offenses, a narrower definition would not be adequate.

Most countries have not defined what computer crime is and how it differs from real-world crime. However, there has been a dramatic increase in specialized legislation to combat these new criminal behaviors. Computer crimes can be charged under at least forty different federal statutes in the United States. The traditional model of law enforcement assumes real-world crime. One characteristic of real-world crime is that the victim and the perpetrator must be in relatively close physical proximity when the crime is committed.

However, in cyberspace there is no crime scene in the traditional sense. For most computer crimes, evidence is scattered over several locations, including the computer the perpetrator used, the victim's computer and the intervening computers and computer servers the perpetrator used to accomplish the offense. Computer crime is not a distinct type of crime, such as rape or murder. Computer crime denotes the use of computer technology to achieve illegal ends. The term "computer crime" includes traditional crimes committed with the use of a computer.

The rapid emergence of computer technologies and the exponential expansion of the Internet have spawned a variety of new, technology-specific criminal behaviors that must also be included in the category of "computer crimes." Computer crime is a borderless crime. It can be committed against a victim who is in another city, another state, or another country. All a perpetrator needs is access to a computer that is linked to the Internet. The perpetrator needs no passport and passes through no checkpoints as he commits his crime. Automation gives perpetrators the ability to commit many computer crimes very quickly. The constraints that govern action in the physical world do not restrict the perpetrators of computer crime.

Computer crime essentially encompasses two types of unlawful activity. First, computer-related crime consists of conduct that targets a computer or a computer system. Attacks on networks, including hacking, denial of service attacks, and virus dissemination, fall into this category. In this category, the computer is akin to the pedestrian who is mugged or the house that is robbed - it is the subject of the attack and the site of any damage caused. Second, computer-enabled crime is a traditional crime like fraud or theft that is facilitated by a computer. A computer may be an "instrument" used to commit traditional crimes such as identity theft, child pornography, copyright infringement, and mail or wire fraud.

Code on Peace, Justice and Security in Cyberspace - A Global Treaty on Cybersecurity and Cybercrime

Recalling the United Nations Convention against Transnational Organized Crime, adopted by General Assembly Resolution 55/25 in 2000, promoting international cooperation to more effectively prevent and combat transnational organized crime, Recalling the United Nations Resolutions 55/63 in 2000 and 56/121 in 2001 on Combating the criminal misuse of information technologies, in which it invited Member States to take into account measures to combat the criminal misuse of information technologies, Recognizing that the free flow of information in cyberspace can promote economic and social development, education and democratic governance,

Noting that the rapid growth of the information and communication technology (ICTs) networks in cyberspace has created new opportunities for criminals in perpetrating crime, and to exploit online vulnerabilities and attack countries' critical information infrastructure, Expressing concern that the technological developments in cyberspace have created new needs for cybersecurity measures in protecting against criminal activity and are cyberthreats of critical concerns to the global society, Noting that the developments of information and communication technologies in cyberspace has resulted in substantial increase in global cooperation and coordination, such that criminal activity may have a grave impact on all States,

Recognizing that differences in levels of information and communication technologies can diminish the effectiveness of international cooperation in combating the criminal activity in cyberspace, and recognizing the need for effective cybersecurity measures, in particular to developing countries, and the need for cooperation between States and the private sector, Noting the necessity of preventing against criminal activities by adequate cybeRecognizing with appreciation the work of the United Nations Office of Drugs and Crime (UNODC) in Vienna, and the outstanding workshops on computer crime and cybercrime at the United Nations Congresses on Crime Prevention and Criminal Justice in Bangkok in 2005 and Salvador, Brazil in 2010, Underlining the need for a common understanding of cybersecurity and cybercrime among countries at all stages of economic development, and establish a global agreement or Protocol at the United Nations level that includes solutions aimed at addressing the global challenges, that may promote peace and security in cyberspace, including legal frameworks that are globally applicable and interoperable with the existing national and regional legislative measures, Recognizing with appreciation the work of the World Summit on the Information Society (WSIS) that in its Tunis Agenda (2005) adopted the following goals:

We affirm that measures undertaken to ensure Internet stability and security, to fight cybercrime and to counter spam, must protect and respect the provisions for privacy and freedom of expression as contained in the relevant parts of the Universal Declaration of Human Rights and the Geneva Declaration of Principles. (Paragraph 42) We call upon governments in cooperation with other stakeholders to develop necessary legislation for the investigation and prosecution of cybercrime, noting existing frameworks, for example, UNGA Resolutions 55/63 and 56/121 on "Combating the criminal misuse of information technologies" and regional initiatives including, but not limited to, the Council of Europe's Convention on Cybercrime. (Paragraph 40)

Welcoming the work of Plenipotentiary Conference in 2006 organized by the International Telecommunication Union (ITU), Recognizing with appreciation the work of the Global Cybersecurity Agenda (GCA) launched by the ITU in 2007 and the strategic proposals from the High Level Experts Group (HLEG), a global expert group of more than 100 experts, that delivered Recommendations in The Chairman's Report and The Global Strategic Report in 2008, including strategies in the following five work areas: Legal Measures, Technical and Procedural Measures, Organizational Structures, Capacity Building, and International Cooperation,

Underlining the need for coordination and cooperation among States in the combat against cybercrime, and emphasize the role that can be played by the United Nations 3 as described in the Salvador Declaration Article 42 (2010), and other international and regional organizations,

Noting the work of international and regional organizations, including the work of the Council of Europe in elaborating the Convention on Cybercrime (2001) and those other organizations in promoting dialogue between government and the private sector on security measures in cyberspace, since cyberthreats are global problems and need a global harmonization involving all stakeholders, Underlining the need for strategies on the development of a Treaty for cybersecurity and cybercrime that may serve as a global model cybersecurity and cybercrime legislation that is applicable and interoperable with existing national and regional legislative measures.

Article 1 – Definitions For the purpose of the Treaty, legal definitions shall be enacted and implemented in accordance with Each Party legal system and practice.

Article 2 – Illegal access Each Party shall adopt such legislative and other measures as may be necessary to establish as criminal offences under its domestic law, when committed intentionally, the access to the whole or any part of a computer system without right. A Party may require that the offence be committed by infringing security measures, with the intent of obtaining computer data or other dishonest intent, or in relation to a computer system that is connected to another computer system.

Article 3 – Illegal interception Each Party shall adopt such legislative and other measures as may be necessary to establish as criminal offences under its domestic law, when committed intentionally, the interception without right, made by technical means, of non-public transmissions of computer data to, from or within a computer system, including electromagnetic emissions from a computer system carrying such computer data. A Party may require that the offence be committed with dishonest intent, or in relation to a computer system that is connected to another computer system.

Article 4 – Data interference

1. Each Party shall adopt such legislative and other measures as may be necessary to establish as criminal offences under its domestic law, when committed intentionally, the damaging, deletion, deterioration, alteration or suppression of computer data without right.

2. A Party may reserve the right to require that the conduct described in paragraph 1 result in serious harm.

Article 5 – System interference Each Party shall adopt such legislative and other measures as may be necessary to establish as criminal offences under its domestic law, when committed intentionally, the serious hindering without right of the functioning of a computer system by inputting, transmitting, damaging, deleting, deteriorating, altering or suppressing computer data.

Article 6 – Misuse of devices

1. Each Party shall adopt such legislative and other measures as may be necessary to establish as criminal offences under its domestic law, when committed intentionally and without right:

a. the production, sale, procurement for use, import, distribution or otherwise

making available of:

i. a device, including a computer program, designed or adapted primarily for the purpose of committing any of the offences established in accordance with the above Articles 2 through 5;

ii. a computer password, access code, or similar data by which the whole or any part of a computer system is capable of being accessed, with intent that it be used for the purpose of committing any of the offences established in Articles 2 through 5; and

b. the possession of an item referred to in paragraphs a.i or ii above, with intent that it be used for the purpose of committing any of the offences established in Articles 2 through 5. A Party may require by law that a number of such items be possessed before criminal liability attaches.

2. This article shall not be interpreted as imposing criminal liability where the production, sale, procurement for use, import, distribution or otherwise making available or possession referred to

in paragraph 1 of this article is not for the purpose of committing an offence established in accordance with Articles 2 through 5 of this Treaty, such as for the authorised testing or protection of a computer system.

3. Each Party may reserve the right not to apply paragraph 1 of this article, provided that the reservation does not concern the sale, distribution or otherwise making available of the items referred to in paragraph 1 a.ii of this article.

Article 7 – Computer-related forgery

Each Party shall adopt such legislative and other measures as may be necessary to establish as criminal offences under its domestic law, when committed intentionally and without right, the input, alteration, deletion, or suppression of computer data, resulting in inauthentic data with the intent that it be considered or acted upon for legal purposes as if it were authentic, regardless whether or not the data is directly readable and intelligible. A Party may require an intent to defraud, or similar dishonest intent, before criminal liability attaches.

Article 8 – Computer-related fraud

Each Party shall adopt such legislative and other measures as may be necessary to establish as criminal offences under its domestic law, when committed intentionally and without right, the causing of a loss of property to another person by:

a. any input, alteration, deletion or suppression of computer data;

b. any interference with the functioning of a computer system, with fraudulent or dishonest intent of procuring, without right, an economic benefit for oneself or for another person.

Article 9 – Offences related to child pornography

1. Each Party shall adopt such legislative and other measures as may be necessary to establish as criminal offences under its domestic law, when committed intentionally and without right, the following conduct:

a. producing child pornography for the purpose of its distribution through a computer system;

b. offering or making available child pornography through a computer system;

c. distributing or transmitting child pornography through a computer system;

d. procuring child pornography through a computer system for oneself or for another person;

e. possessing child pornography in a computer system or on a computer-data storage medium.

2. For the purpose of paragraph 1 above, the term "child pornography" shall include pornographic material that visually depicts:

a. a minor engaged in sexually explicit conduct;

b. a person appearing to be a minor engaged in sexually explicit conduct;

c. realistic images representing a minor engaged in sexually explicit conduct.

3. For the purpose of paragraph 2 above, the term "minor" shall include all persons under 18 years of age. A Party may, however, require a lower age-limit, which shall be not less than 16 years.

4. Each Party may reserve the right not to apply, in whole or in part, paragraphs 1, sub-paragraphs d. and e, and 2, sub-paragraphs b. and c.

Article 10 - Identity Theft

Each Party shall adopt such legislative and other measures as may be necessary to establish as criminal offences under its domestic law, when committed intentionally, the transfer, possession, or use, without right, a means of identification of another person with the intent to commit, or to aid or abet, or in connection with, any unlawful activity that constitutes a violation of law, or acts with the identity of another or with an identity that easily may be confused with the identity of another person, with the intent of

a) procuring an economic benefit for oneself or for another person, or

b) causing a loss of property or inconvenience to another person.

Article 11 - Massive and Coordinated Cyberattacks against Critical Communications and Information Infrastructures

Each Party shall adopt such legislative and other measures as may be necessary to establish as criminal offences under its domestic law, when committed intentionally and without right, whoever by destroying, damaging, or rendering unusable critical communications and information infrastructures, causes substantial and comprehensive disturbance to the national security, civil defence, public administration and services, public health or safety, or banking and financial services.

Article 12 – Prevention of Terrorism and most serious Cyberattacks

Each Party shall adopt such legislative and other measures as may be necessary to establish as criminal offences under its domestic law, when committed intentionally,

1. Public provocation to commit a terrorist offence

1.1. For the purposes of this Treaty, "public provocation to commit a terrorist offence" means the distribution, or otherwise making available, of a message to the public, with the intent to incite the commission of a terrorist offence, where such conduct, whether or not directly advocating terrorist offences, causes a danger that one or more such offences may be committed.

1.2. Each Party shall adopt such measures as may be necessary to establish public provocation to commit a terrorist offence, as defined in paragraph 1, when committed unlawfully and intentionally, as a criminal offence under its domestic law.

2. Recruitment for terrorism

2.1. For the purposes of this Treaty, "recruitment for terrorism" means to solicit another person to commit or participate in the commission of a terrorist offence, or to join an association or group, for the purpose of contributing to the commission of one or more terrorist offences by the association or the group.

2.2. Each Party shall adopt such measures as may be necessary to establish recruitment for terrorism, as defined in paragraph 1, when committed unlawfully and intentionally, as a criminal offence under its domestic law.

3. Training for terrorism

3.1. For the purposes of this Treaty, "training for terrorism" means to provide instruction in the making or use of explosives, firearms or other weapons or noxious or hazardous substances, or in other specific methods or techniques, for the purpose of carrying out or contributing to the commission of a terrorist offence or, knowing that the skills provided are intended to be used for this purpose.

3.2. Each Party shall adopt such measures as may be necessary to establish training for terrorism, as defined in paragraph 1, when committed unlawfully and intentionally, as a criminal offence under its domestic law.

4. The provisions in his section shall also apply on the most serious cyberattacks described in Article 11 on Massive and Coordinated Cyberattacks against Critical Communications and Information Infrastructures

Article 13 - Preparatory acts

1. Each Party shall adopt such legislative and other measures as may be necessary to establish as criminal offences under its domestic law, when committed intentionally, without right, the preparation of an information or communication technology tool or condition, that is especially suitable to commit a cybercrime.

2. Each Party may reserve the right not to apply paragraph 1 of this article, provided that the reservation does not concern the sale, distribution or otherwise making available of the items referred to in this article.

MEASURES IN PROCEDURAL LAW FOR THE INVESTIGATION AND PROSECUTION

Article 14 – Scope of procedural provisions

1. Each Party shall adopt such legislative and other measures as may be necessary to establish the powers and procedures provided

for in this section for the purpose of specific criminal investigations or proceedings.

2. Except as specifically provided otherwise in Article 21, each Party shall apply the powers and procedures referred to in paragraph 1 of this article to:

a. the criminal offences established in accordance with Articles 2 through 13 of this Treaty;

b. other criminal offences committed by means of a computer system; and

c. the collection of evidence in electronic form of a criminal offence.

3.

a. Each Party may reserve the right to apply the measures referred to in

Article 20 only to offences or categories of offences specified in the reservation, provided that the range of such offences or categories of offences is not more restricted than the range of offences to which it applies the measures referred to in Article 21. Each Party shall consider restricting such a reservation to enable the broadest application of the measure referred to in Article 20.

b. Where a Party, due to limitations in its legislation in force at the time of the adoption of the present Treaty, is not able to apply the measures referred to in Articles 20 and 21 to communications being transmitted within a computer system of a service provider, which system:

i. is being operated for the benefit of a closed group of users, and

ii. does not employ public communications networks and is not connected with another computer system, whether public or private, that Party may reserve the right not to apply these measures to such communications. Each Party shall consider restricting such a reservation to enable the broadest application of the measures referred to in Articles 20 and 21.

Article 15 – Conditions and safeguards

1. Each Party shall ensure that the establishment, implementation and application of the powers and procedures provided for in this Section are subject to conditions and safeguards provided for under its domestic law, which shall provide for the adequate protection of human rights and liberties, including rights arising pursuant to obligations it has undertaken under the 1950 Council of Europe Convention for the Protection of Human Rights and Fundamental Freedoms, the 1966 United Nations International Covenant on Civil and Political Rights, and other applicable international human rights instruments, and which shall incorporate the principle of proportionality.

2. Such conditions and safeguards shall, as appropriate in view of the nature of the procedure or power concerned, *inter alia,* include judicial or other independent supervision, grounds justifying application, and limitation of the scope and the duration of such power or procedure.

3. To the extent that it is consistent with the public interest, in particular the sound administration of justice, each Party shall consider the impact of the powers and procedures in this section upon the rights, responsibilities and legitimate interests of third parties.

Article 16 –Expedited preservation of stored computer data

1. Each Party shall adopt such legislative and other measures as may be necessary to enable its competent authorities to order or similarly obtain the expeditious preservation of specified computer data, including traffic data, that has been stored by means of a computer system, in particular where there are grounds to believe that the computer data is particularly vulnerable to loss or modification.

2. Where a Party gives effect to paragraph 1 above by means of an order to a person to preserve specified stored computer data in the person's possession or control, the Party shall adopt such legislative and other measures as may be necessary to oblige that person to preserve and maintain the integrity of that computer data for a period of time as long as necessary, up to a maximum of ninety days, to enable the competent authorities to seek its disclosure. A Party may provide for such an order to be subsequently renewed.

3. Each Party shall adopt such legislative and other measures as may be necessary to oblige the custodian or other person who is to preserve the computer data to keep confidential the undertaking of such procedures for the period of time provided for by its domestic law.

4. The powers and procedures referred to in this article shall be subject to Articles 14 and 15.

Article 17 – Expedited preservation and partial disclosure of traffic data

1. Each Party shall adopt, in respect of traffic data that is to be preserved under Article 16, such legislative and other measures as may be necessary to:

a. ensure that such expeditious preservation of traffic data is available regardless of whether one or more service providers were involved in the transmission of that communication; and

b. ensure the expeditious disclosure to the Party's competent authority, or a person designated by that authority, of a sufficient amount of traffic data to enable the Party to identify the service providers and the path through which the communication was transmitted.

2. The powers and procedures referred to in this article shall be subject to Articles 14 and 15.

Article 18 – Production order

1. Each Party shall adopt such legislative and other measures as may be necessary to empower its competent authorities to order:

a. a person in its territory to submit specified computer data in that person's possession or control, which is stored in a computer system or a computer data storage medium; and

b. a service provider offering its services in the territory of the Party to submit subscriber information relating to such services in that service provider's possession or control.

2. The powers and procedures referred to in this article shall be subject to Articles 14 and 15.

3. For the purpose of this article, the term "subscriber information" means any information contained in the form of computer data or any other form that is held by a service provider, relating to subscribers of its services other than traffic or content data and by which can be established:

a. he type of communication service used, the technical provisions taken thereto and the period of service;

b. the subscriber's identity, postal or geographic address, telephone and other access number, billing and payment information, available on the basis of the service agreement or arrangement;

c. any other information on the site of the installation of communication equipment, available on the basis of the service agreement or arrangement.

Article 19 – Search and seizure of stored computer data

1. Each Party shall adopt such legislative and other measures as may be necessary to empower its competent authorities to search or similarly access:

a. a computer system or part of it and computer data stored therein; and

b. a computer-data storage medium in which computer data may be stored in its territory.

2. Each Party shall adopt such legislative and other measures as may be necessary to ensure that where its authorities search or similarly access a specific computer system or part of it, pursuant to paragraph 1.a, and have grounds to believe that the data sought is stored in another computer system or part of it in its territory, and such data is lawfully accessible from or available to the initial system, the authorities shall be able to expeditiously extend the search or similar accessing to the other system.

3. Each Party shall adopt such legislative and other measures as may be necessary to empower its competent authorities to seize or similarly secure computer data accessed according to paragraphs 1 or 2. These measures shall include the power to:

a. seize or similarly secure a computer system or part of it or a computer-data storage medium;

b. make and retain a copy of those computer data;

c. maintain the integrity of the relevant stored computer data;

d. render inaccessible or remove those computer data in the accessed computer system.

4. Each Party shall adopt such legislative and other measures as may be necessary to empower its competent authorities to order any person who has knowledge about the functioning of the computer system or measures applied to protect the computer data therein to provide, as is reasonable, the necessary information, to enable the undertaking of the measures referred to in paragraphs 1 and 2.

5. The powers and procedures referred to in this article shall be subject to Articles 14 and 15.

Article 20 – Real-time collection of traffic data

1. Each Party shall adopt such legislative and other measures as may be necessary to empower its competent authorities to:

a. collect or record through the application of technical means on the territory of that Party, and

b. compel a service provider, within its existing technical capability:

i. to collect or record through the application of technical means on the territory of that Party; or

ii. to co-operate and assist the competent authorities in the collection or recording of, traffic data, in real-time, associated with specified communications in its territory transmitted by means of a computer system.

2. Where a Party, due to the established principles of its domestic legal system, cannot adopt the measures referred to in paragraph 1.a, it may instead adopt legislative and other measures as

may be necessary to ensure the real-time collection or recording of traffic data associated with specified communications transmitted in its territory, through the application of technical means on that territory.

3. Each Party shall adopt such legislative and other measures as may be necessary to oblige a service provider to keep confidential the fact of the execution of any power provided for in this article and any information relating to it.

4. The powers and procedures referred to in this article shall be subject to Articles 14 and 15.

Article 21 – Interception of content data

1. Each Party shall adopt such legislative and other measures as may be necessary, in relation to a range of serious offences to be determined by domestic law, to empower its competent authorities to:

a. collect or record through the application of technical means on the territory of that Party, and

b. compel a service provider, within its existing technical capability:

i. to collect or record through the application of technical means on the territory of that Party, or

ii. to co-operate and assist the competent authorities in the collection or recording of, content data, in real-time, of specified communications in its territory transmitted by means of a computer system.

2. Where a Party, due to the established principles of its domestic legal system, cannot adopt the measures referred to in paragraph 1.a, it may instead adopt legislative and other measures as may be necessary to ensure the real-time collection or recording of

content data on specified communications in its territory through the application of technical means on that territory.

3. Each Party shall adopt such legislative and other measures as may be necessary to oblige a service provider to keep confidential the fact of the execution of any power provided for in this article and any information relating to it.

4. The powers and procedures referred to in this article shall be subject to Articles 14 and 15.

MEASURES IN GLOBAL JURISDICTION

Article 22 – Jurisdiction

1. Each Party shall adopt such legislative and other measures as may be necessary to establish jurisdiction over any offence established in accordance with Articles 2 through 13 of this Treaty, when the offence is committed:

a. in its territory; or

b. on board a ship flying the flag of that Party; or

c. on board an aircraft registered under the laws of that Party; or

d. by one of its nationals, if the offence is punishable under criminal law where it was committed or if the offence is committed outside the territorial jurisdiction of any State.

2. Each Party may reserve the right not to apply or to apply only in specific cases or conditions the jurisdiction rules laid down in paragraphs 1.b through 1.d of this article or any part thereof.

3. Each Party shall adopt such measures as may be necessary to establish jurisdiction over the offences referred to in Article 2 through 13 of this Treaty, in cases where an alleged offender is present in its territory and it does not extradite him or her to another

Party, solely on the basis of his or her nationality, after a request for extradition.

4. This Treaty does not exclude any criminal jurisdiction exercised by a Party in accordance with its domestic law.

5. When more than one Party claims jurisdiction over an alleged offence established in accordance with this Treaty, the Parties involved shall, where appropriate, consult with a view to determining the most appropriate jurisdiction for prosecution.

Article 23 – General principles relating to international co-operation

The Parties shall co-operate with each other, in accordance with the provisions of this chapter, and through the application of relevant international instruments on international co-operation in criminal matters, arrangements agreed on the basis of uniform or reciprocal legislation, and domestic laws, to the widest extent possible for the purposes of investigations or proceedings concerning criminal offences related to computer systems and data, or for the collection of evidence in electronic form of a criminal offence.

Part two

MEASURES ON CYBERSECURITY

1. A COMMON PERSPECTIVE

Information security constitutes a driving force for the economic development of regions and must be carried out simultaneously with ICT infrastructure. Benefits from information technology services deployment are dependent upon an accompanying development of ICT infrastructure, sufficient security measures and a legal and regulatory framework.

Cybersecurity in a broad sense, including the legal framework, is critical to attract economic actors for developing a favorable business environment. The *global information society* and *knowledge economy* are constrained by the development and overall acceptance of an international cybersecurity framework. The validity of such a framework or model requires a challenging *multidimensional cybersecurity approach* for everyone – from individuals to organizations and states.

Each actor dealing with an information and communication device, tool or service, for professional or private issues, needs information security. It is true for governmental institutions as for big or small organizations and individuals. The security answer should satisfy particular protection and defense levels requirements, in regards of the actor's need. The end user's perspective and the reason for security should never be forgotten as well as the particular needs for privacy and fundamental human rights protection.

Developing security models and solutions is not enough to protect informational resources. If technical security measures have to be developed and implemented, concomitant legal measures have to exist as well to prevent and deter criminal behaviour that uses pervasive networks as a target of crime (new technology – new crimes) or uses pervasive network as a means to realize a crime (old crime with new technology).

The legal dimension of ICT security should be considered as a global business enabler that will contribute to minimizing criminal opportunities.

For developing countries, attempts to reduce the digital divide through investment in infrastructure only, without taking into account the need for security and control of ICT risks (unsolicited incident, malevolent acts, …), would result in the creation of a security divide as prejudicial for developing countries as the digital divide. It has become imperative that developing countries not only introduce measures to fight against cybercrime, but also control the security of their infrastructure and information technologies departments.

The use of an ICT technological and legal approach, would help not to further widen the digital divide by adding a second "security divide", and to quickly create a reliable infrastructure which meets needs at the international level.

Cybersecurity tools and legal framework constitute an additional challenge for developing countries. It is the responsibility of developed countries to help developing countries find their own good practices by transferring knowledge and skills.

It is everyone's responsibility to promote a safe and reliable cyberspace environment in the context of an emerging information society. A minimum level of security for information and communication technologies must be provided at an affordable cost. Security must not become an exclusion factor for anyone who would like to conduct private or business activities over the Internet.

CHAPTER FIVE
CYBERCRIME AND COMPUTER CRIME LEGISLATION

Cybercrime law includes laws related to computer crime, internet crime, information crimes, communications crimes and technology crimes. While the internet and the digital economy represent a significant opportunity, it is also an enabler for criminal activity. Cybercrime law is laws that create the offences and penalties for cybercrimes. Cybercrime describes both:

- Crimes directed at computers, data or information communications technologies (ICTs), and
- Crimes committed by people using computers or ICT.

Cybercrime is a global problem, which requires a coordinated international response.

Many laws around the world were enacted to combat computer crime and cybercrime. They include:

International cybercrime conventions

- African Union Convention on Cyberspace Security and Personal Data Protection
- Council of Europe Convention on Cybercrime (also known as the Budapest Convention on Cybercrime)

Model Laws

- CW Model Law – Model Law on Computer and Computer-related Crime
- SADC Model Law – SADC Model Law on Computer Crime and Cybercrime

- HIPCAR – Harmonization of ICT Policies, Legislation and Regulatory Procedures in the Caribbeans (Cybercrime/e-Crimes)
- ITU – International Telecommunications Union Cybercrime Legislation Resources – ITU Toolkit for Cybercrime Legislation

Some specific cybercrime law

- Cybercrimes and Cybersecurity Bill (Cyber Bill) – South Africa (South Africa signed the Budapest Convention in 2001)
- Cybersecurity Information Sharing Act (CISA) – United States of America (this Bill has recently been passed by the US Senate)
- EU Network and Information Security Directive
- Criminal Code Act 1995 Australia
- Cybercrime Act 2001 Australia
- Chapter 08:06 (Cybercrime and Computer- related Crimes) Botswana
- Computer Misuse Act, 2007 Brunei Darussalam
- Criminal Code of Canada
- Cybersecurity Law China
- Criminal Code France
- Computer Crimes Act Malaysia
- Crimes Act,1961 New Zealand
- Cybercrime Prevention Act of 2012 – Philippines
- Act on Computer Crimes Thailand
- Cybercrimes Act, 2015 Tanzania
- UK – Computer Misuse Act, 2013

- United States Code USA

African Union Convention on Cyberspace Security and Personal Data Protection

The Cybercrimes and Cybersecurity Bill is in the process of being enacted. Some people will call it the Cyber Bill, Cybercrime Bill or Cybercrime Act. Others might refer to it as the CaC Bill or just CaC. What will you call it?

The second draft of the Cyber Bill is still tabled in Parliament and we have studied it (all 139 pages of it) so that you don't have to. We provide you with an overview below. Why is it necessary? Who is affected? What action do you need to take? Should you be commenting on it? What does it deal with? We answer these questions in this article.

This is a scary and bad law that has severe consequences if you don't comply. Attend our full day Cyber Crime and Security Workshop to get a deeper understanding of the impact on your organization.

Why do we need the Cyber Bill?

Many people will be asking – Do we need the Cybercrime Bill? Cybercrime is on the increase and the Cybercrimes and Cybersecurity Bill aims to keep people safe from criminals, terrorists and other states. It also consolidates cybercrime laws into one place. Essentially, it aims to stop cybercrime and improve the security of the country.

Who is affected by the Cybercrimes and Cybersecurity Bill?

The practical impact of the Cyber Bill on all organizations and all individuals is significant and unfortunately mostly negative. We thought it had been fixed but it hasn't. Law enforcement wants to curtail our freedom by making everyday things a crime. It impacts all of us who process data or use a computer. Individuals, parents, journalists, organizations, banks and many others will probably commit many offences daily.

- People involved with IT (or data protection) regulatory compliance.
- All Electronic Communications Service Providers (ECSPs).
- Financial institutions.
- Representatives from various government departments.
- Cyber criminals and terrorists.
- Providers or vendors of software or hardware tools that could be used to commit offences.
- Information security experts.
- Anyone who owns an Information Infrastructure that government could declare as critical.
- Everyone who uses a computer or the internet.
- The Police Service.

Possible actions for you to take

1. Attend a public Cyber Crime and Security Workshop.
2. Arrange for your own private in-house Cyber Crime and Security Workshop.
3. Brief your board on cyber security risks and the legal implications for your organisation.

4. Read the 2017 version of the Bill and its related CyberCrimes Discussion Document 2017 .
5. Send this article to someone else you think might be interested.
6. Subscribe to the Michalsons newsletter to receive future updates.

The timeline on the Cybercrime Bill

The Cybercrime Bill was first published on 28 August 2015, updated on 19 January 2017 and was introduced in Parliament on 22 February 2017. The bill is still sitting at Parliament as there was a strong push by the old regime in government to enact the Bill in its then-current form. There were extensive comments on the Bill during the public participation period in 2017, and particularly on onerous aspects of the Bill. Those comments will hopefully be considered and some incorporated into the Bill before it becomes law.

Overview of the latest version of the Cyber Bill

The Cybercrime Bill creates many new offences. Some are related to data, messages, computers, and networks. For example:

- hacking,
- unlawful interception of data,
- ransomware,
- cyber forgery and uttering, or
- Cyber extortion.

The penalties consist of a fine, imprisonment, or both. How much could you be fined? The Bill no longer specifies this, but if you are convicted of a cybercrime, you could spend between one year to fifteen years in prison, depending on the cybercrime. The Cybercrime Bill gives the courts jurisdiction to try these offences is some cases where there is uncertainty.

The National Director of Public Prosecutions must keep statistics on the number, and results of prosecutions for cybercrimes. These statistics must be included in the NDPP's report on the NPA.

The Cybercrimes and Cybersecurity Bill gives the Police Service (and their members and investigators) extensive powers to investigate, search, access and seize just about anything (like a computer, database or network) wherever it might be located, provided they have a search warrant. Foreign states will co-operate to investigate cybercrimes.

To deal with cybercrime, the Minister of Police must establish and maintain:

- a 24/7 Point of Contact for cyber crimes, and
- the capacity to detect, prevent and investigate cybercrimes.

To improve Cyber Security, the Cybercrimes and Cybersecurity Bill creates a Cyber Response Committee. The function of the Cyber Response Committee is to implement Government policy relating to cybersecurity. The chairperson will be the Director-General: State Security, and the Minister of State Security will oversee and exercise control over the Cyber Response Committee.

The Minister of State Security must establish and operate a Computer Security Incident Response Team (CSIRT) for Government, and ensure that there are enough people to deal with critical infrastructure protection.

The Minister of Defence must establish and maintain a cyber offensive and defensive capacity as part of the Defence Force's mandate.

The Minister of Telecommunications and Postal Services must establish and maintain a Cyber Security Hub that:

- promotes cybersecurity in the private sector,
- acts as a central point of contact between Government and the private sector on cybersecurity,
- helps establish nodal points and Private Sector Computer Security Incident Response Teams (PSCSIRT) in different sectors, and
- Responds to cybersecurity incidents.

The Bill aims to identify, declare and protect Critical Information Infrastructures, like the Department of Home Affairs database. There are various obligations on the owner of (or person in control of) Critical Information Infrastructure.

The Cybercrime Bill helps people to admit evidence of cybercrimes.

ECSPs and financial institutions must:

- report offences to the police no later than 72 hours,
- preserve any information that relates to it.

If an ECSP or a financial institution doesn't, it is liable on conviction to a fine of R50 000.

This does not mean that ESCPs and financial institutions have to monitor the data they transmit or store on their systems. They also don't have to actively look for situations that indicate unlawful activity.

The Cybercrime Bill enables the Minister of Justice to make regulations on information sharing. This includes sharing information on cybersecurity incidents, detecting, preventing and investigating cybercrimes.

The President may enter into agreements with other states considering this is a global issue.

Various laws are repealed or amended, most notably Chapter 9 and sections 85, 86, 87, 88 and 90 of the ECT Act.

CONCLUSION

The future of the Internet is still up for grabs between criminals and normal users. Fears of a cyber apocalypse still abound, while the potential extent of damage that can be caused by wide scale fraud is nearly unbounded. These anxieties should be rationally tempered with the knowledge that the problems are being addressed, although perhaps not fast enough. The usefulness of the Internet has proved itself in numerous and myriad ways that will hopefully be enough to ensure it does not become a wasteland of criminal activity and a bastion for the malicious.

The government still has an important role to play, but most of the prevention needs to be done by commercial entities producing software and those with the ability to stop fraud. Relying on consumer education programs will only affect a percentage of possible victims. The others need to be automatically protected through measures that do not stress and require considerable participation. Security needs to be easy and effective if it is doing work. Whether cybercrime is still a pertinent issue ten years from now is unknowable in a sense, but if the Internet will continue to grow, it must be solved so that the realities of cybercrime will be proportional to real-world crimes, if not better.

REFERENCES

- Gercke, Marco: National, Regional and International Approaches in the Fight against Cybercrime, CRi 2008.
- Gercke, Marco: The Convention on Cybercrime, MMR (2004).
- Schjolberg and Hubbard: Harmonizing National Legal Approaches on Cybercrime (2005).
- Schjolberg, Stein: Terrorism in Cyberspace – Myth or Reality? (2007) www.cybercrimelaw.net
- Schjolberg, Stein: Wanted: A United Nations Cyberspace Treaty - Global Cyber Deterrence (2010) – www.ewi.info.
- Schjolberg, Stein: A Cyberspace Treaty – A United Nations Convention or Protocol on Cybersecurity and Cybercrime, 12th United Nations Congress on Crime Prevention and Criminal Justice (2010) – www.cybercrimelaw.net
- Schjolberg, Stein: Global Supreme Court decisions – www.globalcourts.com
- Sieber, Ulrich: Council of Europe Organised Crime Report (2004).
- Sieber and Brunst: Cyberterrorism and Other Use of the Internet for Terroris Purposes – Threat Analysis and Evaluation of International Conventions (2007).

- Sieber, Ulrich: Cybercrime and Jurisdiction in Germany. The Present Situation and the Need for New Solutions, (2006).
- Sofaer and Goodman: Cyber Crime and Security - The Transnational Dimension of Cyber Crime and Security (2008).
- Wilson, Clay: Botnets, Cybercrime, and Cyberterrorism: Vulnerabilities and Policy Issues for Congress, CRS Report for US Congress (November 2007)
- https://www.linkedin.com/pulse/scope-various-international-legal-instruments-cyber-world-sharma
- GLOBAL NATURE OF COMPUTER CRIMES AND THE CONVENTION ON CYBERCRIME
http://dergiler.ankara.edu.tr/dergiler/64/1541/16889.pdf
- United Nations Intergovernmental Expert Group on Cybercrime Vienna, 3-5 April 2018 Panel on legislation and legal frameworks Legislation and legal frameworks on cybercrime and electronic evidence: Some comments on developments 2013 – 2018
Cristina Schulman Ministry of Justice, Romania
http://www.unodc.org/documents/organizedcrime/cybercrime/cybercrime-april-2018/SCHULMAN_Item_2.pdf

www.ingramcontent.com/pod-product-compliance
Lightning Source LLC
Chambersburg PA
CBHW030449220526
45464CB00006B/2454